the DOUBLE LOVE DEVOTIONAL

A 40-day Devotional Designed to Help You Grow Your Love for God and People

DEMETRIUS McCRAY

The Double Love Devotional: A 40-day Devotional
Designed to Help You Grow Your Love for God and People

Published by: Demetrius McCray

All Scripture quotations, unless otherwise indicated, are taken from the Holy Bible, New International Version®, NIV®. Copyright ©1973, 1978, 1984, 2011 by Biblica, Inc.™ Used by permission of Zondervan. All rights reserved worldwide. www.zondervan.com The "NIV" and "New International Version" are trademarks registered in the United States Patent and Trademark Office by Biblica, Inc.™

Copyright © 2025 Demetrius McCray

ISBN: 979-8-218-65372-9

Editing by Demetrius McCray
Front cover image by Marvin Eans
Book design (Interior) by Marvin Eans

All rights reserved. No part of this book may be reproduced in any form or by any electronic or mechanical means, including information storage and retrieval systems, without permission in writing from the publisher, except by reviewers, who may quote brief passages in a review.

Printed and bound in the United States of America
First printing July 2025

DEDICATION

Before we begin the journey, I want to share with you a little about myself.

I am three years married to the love of my life, Lauren. She is truly a blessing! For most of our marriage, we both worked as teachers at a Christian school in Florida. After eight years of teaching, I recently decided to step away from that role to pursue a PhD in Bible Exposition from Liberty University. However, I miss getting to disciple my former students from Calvary Christian Academy in Ormond Beach, Florida, that is why I have written this devotional. It is my passion and part of my life's assignment to teach and disciple the next generation of Jesus followers through my writing!

This devotional is dedicated to my wife, all of my former students, and the body of Christ. May anyone who reads *The Double Love Devotional* come to know and show the love of God in a personal way!

CONTENTS

07 **INTRODUCTION**

08 **LOVED BY GOD
SECTION 1**

08 DAY 1 | He Started It!

12 DAY 2 | There's More!

16 **LOVE FOR GOD
SECTION 2**

16 DAY 3 | The Greatest Commandment

20 DAY 4 | "no other gods"

24 DAY 5 | You Can't Sit Here

28 DAY 6 | Agree to Disagree

32 DAY 7 | A Deal-breaker

36 DAY 8 | Believe Me When I Tell You.

40 DAY 9 | Louder Than Words

44 DAY 10 | "God as My Witness?"

48 **DAY 11 | You're in Debt!
LOVE FOR PEOPLE
SECTION 3**

52 DAY 12 | Do Not Murder

56 DAY 13 | Keep The Knot

60 DAY 14 | Stealing

64 DAY 15 | Do Not Give False Testimony

68 DAY 16 | Do Not Covet

72 DAY 17 | Like You Mean It!

76 DAY 18 | Bless You!

80 DAY 19 | Poke the Bear

84 DAY 20 | "I'll Pray for You"

CONTENTS

- **88** DAY 21 | Forgive One Another
- **92** DAY 22 | Encouragement
- **96** DAY 23 | Sticks and Stones!
- **100** DAY 24 | Love on the Streets
- **104** DAY 25 | Hit the Share Button!
- **108** DAY 26 | You Should be Religious.
- **112** DAY 27 | What About my Enemies?
- **116** DAY 28 | Peace Out
- **120** DAY 29 | Tell the Truth!
- **124** DAY 30 | Love God and Love People
- **128** WHY 40?
- **130 DAY 31 | These Things! SECTION 4**
- **134** DAY 32 | Lavishly Loved
- **138** DAY 33 | God's Children's Love
- **142** DAY 34 | God's Children's Love Pt. 2
- **146** DAY 35 | Mutual Indwelling Pt. 1
- **150** DAY 36 | Mutual Indwelling Pt. 2
- **154** DAY 37 | Spiritual Certainties
- **158** DAY 38 | Continuation in Community
- **162** DAY 39 | Sin Less and be Sinless
- **166** DAY 40 | "as yourself"
- **170 SELF ASSESSMENT**

INTRODUCTION

Let me start by saying thank you for accepting the invitation to love on another level! I am confident that what you learn from this devotional about biblical love will impact how you see God, yourself, and the people around you.

Recently, I've found myself puzzled by the double love commandment in Matthew 22:37-39. It reads, "Love the Lord your God with all your heart, with all your soul, and with all your mind." Jesus goes on to say that the second command is like the first: "Love your neighbor as yourself." I read this, thinking to myself, "Wait, what?" "How do you command love?" Have you ever thought about this? Isn't the goal of a command to make someone do something? Isn't love something that must be genuine? What if I don't feel like obeying the command? Then it hit me: A command invites a decision: to follow or disregard. You may be thinking, "What does that have to do with love?" My friend, it has everything to do with love! Loving God and your neighbor is not merely an emotion but a daily decision. That is why I have written this devotional. The Double Love Devotional is designed to help you get a clearer picture of biblical love, leading to a deeper love for God and people!

LOVED BY GOD: SECTION 1

DAY 1 – He Started It!

> *"We love because He first loved us."*
> ***1 John 4:19 NIV***

💡 Devotional Thought

Love for God begins with knowing that God loves you. God has proven His love for us by sending Jesus to save us through His crucifixion and resurrection. However, it is not enough for us to simply know that we are loved. God wants us to receive and experience the love He has for us.

We receive God's love by accepting Jesus as Lord and Savior.

> "For God so loved the world that He gave…"
> When someone gives you a gift to express their love for you, receiving the gift is like saying, "I receive your love for me." God indeed loves everyone, but not everyone receives His love.

To reject Jesus is to reject God's love. This does not mean that God stops loving people who reject Jesus, but that they reject the greatest gift given to humanity that communicates His love. God's love for us is meant to awaken our love for Him!

🔍 Reflection

- How has God proven His love for us?

- How do we receive God's love?

> We receive God's love by accepting Jesus as Lord and Savior.

Day 1 Notes:

Day 1 Notes:

LOVED BY GOD: SECTION 1

DAY 2 - There's More!

> *"Whoever has my commands and keeps them is the one who loves me. The one who loves me will be loved by my Father, and I too will love them and show myself to them"* **1 John 4:19 NIV**

💡 Devotional Thought

I remember reading this verse and finding myself a bit confused. "Will be loved by my Father"? Wait, I thought that I was already loved by God according to John 3:16. It was at that point that I knew that I had to dig deeper in my study of this passage. I won't bore some of you with the grammatical and linguistic technicalities, so I will cut straight to the point. During Jesus' farewell address to His disciples, He explained to them what love for Him looks like. Love for Jesus is expressed in accepting and obeying His commands.

As a result, we "will be loved" by the Father. But what does all of this mean? In simple terms, John 3:16 love is God's demonstrated/communicated love, while John 14:21 describes God's love that is experienced through a relationship with Him. In other words, "will be loved" means that God's love becomes personal. His love becomes more real to you than the air you breathe. It is a constant exchange of love. Mutual love!

🔍 Reflection

- How do we express love for God?

- What did Jesus mean by "will be loved by my Father" in John 14:21?

His love becomes more real to you than the air you breathe. It is a constant exchange of love. Mutual love!

Day 2 Notes:

Day 2 Notes:

LOVE FOR GOD: SECTION 2

Day 3 - The Greatest Commandment

> *"Love the Lord your God with all your heart and with all your soul and with all your strength."* **Deuteronomy 6:5**

💡 Devotional Thought

"Stop forcing your religion on me!" Anyone who has attempted to share their faith or explain their biblical stance on a topic has probably heard this statement before. Was this God's intention when He commanded the Israelites to love Him? Was God forcing them to comply or die? How do you command love? How do you command an emotion? The answer is actually quite simple. First, love for God is both a decision and an emotion.

Our attitude toward God should always be loving even if the emotion isn't there initially. When we decide to love God, the emotion develops over time. Soon enough, our love for God starts to show in our loyalty and actions. Loyalty means that we choose Him every time over anyone and anything else. We choose to be loyal to Him in our beliefs and our actions. The words "heart" "soul" and "strength" mean that you love God with every part of your being.

🔍 Reflection

- What is the greatest commandment in the Bible?

- If love is not just an emotion, what else is it?

> Our attitude toward God should always be loving even if the emotion isn't there initially.

Day 3 Notes:

Day 3 Notes:

LOVE FOR GOD: SECTION 2

Day 4 – "No Other gods"

> *"You shall have no other gods before me."* **Deuteronomy 5:7**

💡 Devotional Thought

I once heard it said that "choices are most powerful in the midst of options." Like us, the Israelites had many options. At the time Israel was given this command, they were surrounded by options. The other nations worshipped their own gods because people were very religious in the ancient world. Yahweh's command was a call to Israel to always prefer Him over the other gods. To choose Him in the midst of options.

The world in which we live may not be as religious as the ancient world, but we are still faced with the option to worship other gods. There are religions that worship other gods, and there are things that people worship other than the one true living God. For example, some people choose money, fame, power, or the god of another religion over the God of the Bible. To love God, then, means to choose Him over anyone and anything else. To choose Him is to love Him!

🔍 Reflection

- What does it mean to you personally to "have no other gods" before God?

- What are some ways we can avoid prioritizing other things over God?

Day 4 Notes:

Day 4 Notes:

LOVE FOR GOD: SECTION 2

Day 5 - You Can't Sit Here

> *"You shall have no other gods before me."* ***Deuteronomy 5:7***

Devotional Thought

In some Bible translations, the word "before" is translated as "beside." Well, which is correct? The answer is BOTH! Not only does God want us to prefer Him in the midst of options, but He doesn't want anything or anyone else to be viewed and loved on the same level as Himself. This eventually creates conflict as you will find yourself in moments of having to choose one over the other.

To love God means to worship Him only. In some religions, people worship multiple gods. In the Christian faith, our God teaches us that He is the only god worthy of worship. Non-Christians may find this offensive, but God calls this love for Him. So, we don't worship God along with other gods, nor do we worship God along with money, success, relationships, power, etc. Love for God is undivided loyalty. Nothing and no one else deserves a place next to the true and living God.

Reflection

- Is it biblical to love God along with other gods?

- How does worshiping other things affect our loyalty to God?

> To love God means to
> worship him only.

Day 5 Notes:

Day 5 Notes:

LOVE FOR GOD: SECTION 2

Day 6 – Agree to Disagree

> *"If you love me, keep my commands"* **John 14:15**

💡 Devotional Thought

Have you ever been in a heated debate with someone, and you or the other person responded, "Well, we're just going to have to agree to disagree."? Usually, this response means that one of you recognizes that no matter how much both of you go back and forth, neither of you will convince the other person to agree with you. Well… this doesn't work with God. Agreement with God is another way of loving Him. You may be thinking, "I don't always agree with God, so does this mean that I don't love Him?" Not necessarily, it just means that there are areas in your life where you must humbly give up your opinion.

Anyone who truly loves God will eventually agree with Him even if they don't at first. Has God ever told you to apologize or forgive someone and you didn't want to at first, but eventually you did because he convinced you that you should? That's agreement! That's love! To agree with God is to love God.

🔍 Reflection

- According to today's reading, what is another way of loving God?

- What must we give up to be able to do this?

> To agree with God is to love God.

Day 6 Notes:

Day 6 Notes:

LOVE FOR GOD: SECTION 2

Day 7 – A Deal-breaker

> *"I desire to do your will, my God; your law is within my heart."*
> ***Psalm 40:8***

💡 Devotional Thought

No matter who we are, where we live, or how we were raised, we all have our deal-breakers. A deal-breaker can be defined as something important to you that prevents you from agreeing to something. For example, someone may decline to buy a certain house because it doesn't come with a swimming pool in the backyard, or someone may decide not to date a person who shows signs of a controlling personality.

There are so many examples of deal-breakers. What this means is that all of us have preferences. Sometimes, our preferences get in the way of us expressing our love for God. What preferences are stopping you from agreeing with God? Maybe you prefer to forgive after the person who offended you apologizes. God, on the other hand, could be telling you to forgive whether the other person chooses to apologize or not. To choose God over your deal-breaker/preference in any situation is yet another way to love Him.

🔍 Reflection

- According to today's reading, what is another way of loving God?

- What must we give up to be able to do this?

To choose God over your deal- breaker/ preference in any situation is yet another way to love Him.

Day 7 Notes:

Day 7 Notes:

LOVE FOR GOD: SECTION 2

Day 8 – Believe Me When I Tell You.

> *Do not conform to the pattern of this world, but be transformed by the renewing of your mind.* **Romans 12:2**

💡 Devotional Thought

Christian or not, everyone has a worldview. Everyone sees the world a certain way. A worldview is simply a way of seeing the world around you based on certain beliefs. Some people, for example, believe that there are no good people in the world. Based on this belief, they trust no one and avoid making meaningful social connections.

What if I told you that allowing God's word (the Bible) to tell you what to believe and how to think about certain topics is another way of loving God? For example, Genesis 1:27 and Matthew 19:4 affirm that God has created only two genders. Interestingly enough, Jesus quoted Genesis 1:27 in Matthew 19:4. If you disagree with Jesus on this topic or any other topic, you should ask Him to speak to you about this. As believers, we should believe in God's word that there are only two genders. The world will know who we are most loyal to by what we publicly stand for or against. Love for God is shown and proven by agreeing with Him in our beliefs.

🔍 Reflection

- What is a Christian worldview?

- How does someone's worldview affect their love for God?

> Love for God is shown and proven by agreeing with Him in our beliefs.

Day 8 Notes:

Day 8 Notes:

LOVE FOR GOD: SECTION 2

Day 9 – Louder Than Words

> *Dear children, let us not love with words or speech but with actions and in truth.* **1 John 3:18**

Devotional Thought

Could you imagine if someone told you that they loved you, yet they never showed it? Would you believe them? The truth is actions really do speak louder than words. Genuine love is not only expressed in saying that we love someone but showing them that we love them. We show our love for people by spending time with them, giving them a gift, or even just reaching out to check on them. There are many ways we can express our love for others.

What if God only declared His love for the world but never sent Jesus? Would we believe that He truly loved us? Probably not. God indeed knows our hearts, but we show our love for Him through our actions. We show our love for God by choosing to display godly actions over ungodliness. Our love for Him is seen by others through our godly deeds, behavior, and even our connectivity and participation in a local church.

Reflection

- According to today's reading, what are two ways that we show love to others?

- How do others see that we love God?

> **We show our love for God by choosing to display godly actions over ungodliness.**

Day 9 Notes:

Day 9 Notes:

LOVE FOR GOD: SECTION 2

Day 10 – "God as My Witness?"

> "You shall not misuse the name of the Lord your God, for the Lord will not hold anyone guiltless who misuses his name."
> **Deuteronomy 5:11**

💡 Devotional Thought

How good are you at keeping your word? Isn't it disappointing whenever someone makes you a promise that they never intended to keep? They swore that they would pay you back the money they owed but never did. The people of Israel would swear on the name of God whenever they made an oath or promise. If that promise was not kept, then the Lord's name was taken or spoken in vain. That is what this verse means. In other words, if someone made an oath or promise in the name of God, it had to be kept. However, Jesus not only teaches against swearing falsely, but He commands us not to swear at all. He teaches us to keep our word when he says, "Let your 'Yes' be 'Yes,' and your 'No,' be 'No.'" What does this have to do with loving God? I'm glad you asked! Keeping your word is another way of expressing love for God.

🔍 Reflection

- What does it mean to misuse or take the Lord's name in vain?

- How might you explain this biblical principle to someone who sees nothing wrong with not keeping their word?

> Keeping your word is another way of expressing love for God.

Day 10 Notes:

Day 10 Notes:

LOVE FOR PEOPLE: SECTION 3

Day 11 - You're in Debt!

> *Let no debt remain outstanding, except the continuing debt to love one another, for whoever loves others has fulfilled the law.*
> **Romans 13:8**

💡 Devotional Thought

One thing that any adult or young adult hates is debt. The feeling of owing an outstanding balance can be overwhelmingly stressful. People experience fear, anxiety, and even depression at the thought of not being able to pay off a debt owed. There is such a feeling of relief that comes with paying off a debt. Well… as a believer, you are in debt for the rest of your life. Yes, you read it right! You're in debt! You owe people love! … Even people who hate you.

I must admit that it can be difficult to love people who hate you. So, what do we do? We do what the Bible says! In Matthew 5:44, Jesus tells us to love our enemies and to pray for those who mistreat us. Whether people are easy to love or hard to love, we owe them love. By doing this, we live out the reality that we are God's children.

🔍 Reflection

- According to today's reading, what do we owe people?

- What are some ways that we can love our enemies?

Whether people are easy to love or hard to love, we owe them love.

Day 11 Notes:

Day 11 Notes:

LOVE FOR PEOPLE: SECTION 3

Day 12 – Do not Murder

> *"You shall not murder."* **Deuteronomy 5:17**

💡 Devotional Thought

Whether male or female, all people have been created in the image of God. Therefore, all human beings have equal value. To commit murder is to ignore a person's natural value and choose to unjustly take that person's "God—given right" to live. Whether in the womb or fully grown, life is precious to God. Paul teaches us in Ephesians 4:26 to not allow our anger to cause us to sin.

In an extreme case, anger can lead to taking someone's life. He adds, "Do not let the sun go down while you are still angry." In other words, do not allow yourself to hold on to anger. Anger could cause you to do something that you will eventually regret. Thus, another way to love people is by releasing your anger toward them so that it does not cause you to no longer see their value and do harm to them.

🔍 Reflection

- Do males and females have equal value?

- How should we deal with anger and let love prevail?

> Whether in the womb or fully grown, life is precious to God.

Day 12 Notes:

Day 12 Notes:

LOVE FOR PEOPLE: SECTION 3

Day 13 - Keep The Knot

> *"You shall not commit adultery."* **Deuteronomy 5:18**

💡 Devotional Thought

Christian teens and young adults need a healthy biblical understanding of love, sex, and marriage. In this devotional, we will keep it simple and appropriate. First, marriage is God's idea. Marriage is between a biological male and a biological female. It is the only kind of marriage that God recognizes and blesses. Marriage is sacred. In other words, marriage is special and connected to God.

During a marriage ceremony, the man and woman make promises in front of a crowd of people and God to care for one another and to be faithful to each other. They commit their lives to one another. Part of this commitment involves their bodies. With that being said, sex is for marriage. It is designed for procreation (making babies) and enjoyment only between the husband and wife. Love for one's husband or wife means not giving your body to someone you are not married to. You may not be married now or even thinking about marriage at this stage in life, but just in case you desire to marry in the future, keep this in mind. Tie the knot and keep the knot!

🔍 Reflection

- What kind of marriage does God recognize and bless?

- How might understanding biblical marriage help us love God and others?

> Marriage is special and connected to God.

Day 13 Notes:

Day 13 Notes:

LOVE FOR PEOPLE: SECTION 3

Day 14 - Stealing

> *"You shall not steal."* **Deuteronomy 5:19**

💡 Devotional Thought

The Bible clearly states, "Do not steal." This is more than just some rule that we should avoid breaking. This is another way of loving people. Have you ever asked yourself why people steal? Some people steal for the thrill of it, some because they feel that it is "necessary" for provision, and others simply because they want what someone else has. No matter the reasoning behind it, stealing puts others at a disadvantage, and depending on what is stolen, it can cause mental and emotional pain to them.

Stealing is never justified in the eyes of God, even if the intention is to "take from the rich to give to the poor." At the root of stealing is an ungodly desire for what someone else has and obtaining it in a wrongful manner. I believe that the remedy to stealing is being content with what you do have and trusting God to provide what you don't have.

🔍 Reflection

- In the eyes of God, is it ever right to steal from someone?

- How might a person overcome a desire or habit of stealing?

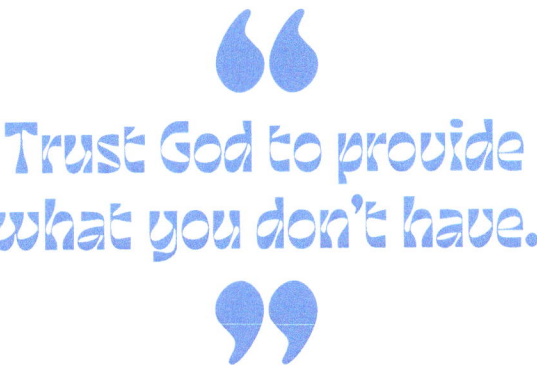

> Trust God to provide what you don't have.

Day 14 Notes:

Day 14 Notes:

LOVE FOR PEOPLE: SECTION 3

Day 15 - Do not Give False Testimony

> *"You shall not give false testimony against your neighbor."*
> **Deuteronomy 5:20**

💡 Devotional Thought

Has anyone ever made up a story to ruin your reputation or to cause you to get in trouble for something that you didn't say or do? This is what it means in the Ten Commandments to "give false testimony against your neighbor." To say that someone said or did something when they didn't. Oftentimes, this happens because someone seeks to be malicious or because they have been bribed into doing so.

A false testimony could potentially put someone else's life in danger. For example, false testimony led to Jesus' suffering and crucifixion. Although Jesus' situation was inevitable, the false testimonies against Him were still wrong. When you truly love your neighbor, you won't make false accusations about them that could result in them getting into serious trouble or being harmed by others. Besides, if the people who believed you found out that you were lying, then you would lose all credibility, and they would no longer trust your word.

🔍 Reflection

- Why should we avoid giving false testimony?

- Was false testimony ever given against Jesus?

When you truly love your neighbor, you won't make false accusations about them that could result in them getting into serious trouble or being harmed by others.

Day 15 Notes:

Day 15 Notes:

LOVE FOR PEOPLE: SECTION 3

Day 16 – Do not Covet

> *"You shall not covet your neighbor's wife. You shall not set your desire on your neighbor's house or land, his male or female servant, his ox or donkey, or anything that belongs to your neighbor."* **Deuteronomy 5:21**

Devotional Thought

Covet? What does that mean? Covet means to have a strong/intense desire for wealth, possessions, or what someone else has. It's possible to covet popularity, social media followers/likes, and even relationships. The danger of covetousness is that you may be willing to do almost anything to get what your neighbor has. This leads to the temptation to either steal what they have or sabotage it because of jealousy.

For example, coveting could look like this: sabotaging a relationship or friendship because you want a certain individual to date you or only be friends with you. So, what is at the root of covetousness? The answer is discontentment. You are not satisfied with what you have. One thing that helps us to be content with what we have is by thanking God for what we do have. Thankfulness is like a weedkiller. It kills weeds of covetousness (intense ungodly desires). Not coveting is loving your neighbor.

Reflection

- What does it mean to covet?

- How does coveting affect our love for God and others?

One thing that helps us to be
content with what we have
is by thanking God for
what we do have.

Day 16 Notes:

Day 16 Notes:

LOVE FOR PEOPLE: SECTION 3

Day 17 – Like You Mean It!

> *Love must be sincere. Hate what is evil; cling to what is good.* **Romans 12:9**

💡 Devotional Thought

I once came across a video of a mom who had her daughter and son put on a single shirt with the words "Get along shirt" written on it. With the daughter's arm through one sleeve and the son's through the other, they were forced to be physically close to one another in the heat of their anger until they calmed down and got along with each other. After both of them reluctantly apologized, they were free to go. They verbalized their apologies but their hostile attitudes remained the same. What's the point?

Although actions speak louder than words, actions can be performed without a genuine attitude of love attached to them. Paul teaches us in Romans 12:9 that "Love must be sincere." Actions may speak louder than words, but attitude verifies the legitimacy of both words and actions. In other words, your attitude communicates to people if you actually mean what you say or do. Love today like you mean it!

🔍 Reflection

- According to today's reading, what must accompany our actions?

- What does Paul say about love in Romans 12:9?

"Love today like you mean it!"

Day 17 Notes:

Day 17 Notes:

LOVE FOR PEOPLE: SECTION 3

Day 18 - Bless You!

> *Bless those who persecute you; bless and do not curse.*
> **Romans 12:14**

💡 Devotional Thought

Whenever someone sneezes, we typically respond with "Bless you!" Why do we do that? I don't know… Someone may argue, "Because it's the respectful thing to do!" Yeah but… Never mind… Whether we agree that it's necessary or not, it's a thing. At least it is here in America. Blessing people is not reserved for a sneeze. Paul teaches us in Romans 12:14 that we are to bless those who persecute us. Persecution is what comes with being a Christian. In fact, Jesus teaches us that we will be persecuted for righteousness sake (Matthew 5:10). This means that there will be people who persecute us because we choose to live according to God's will in purpose, thought, and action. Our response is not to curse them, but to bless them. Blessing those who persecute you is another way of loving people. Those who persecute you are also your neighbors. What does it mean to "bless" them? It means to genuinely pray for God's best for them.

🔍 Reflection

- What are we instructed to do to those who persecute us?

- What does our response to persecution have to do with our love for God and others?

> Blessing those who persecute you is another way of loving people.

Day 18 Notes:

Day 18 Notes:

LOVE FOR PEOPLE: SECTION 3

Day 19 - Poke the Bear

> *And let us consider how we may spur one another on toward love and good deeds.* **Hebrews 10:24**

💡 Devotional Thought

It's probably not a good idea to poke a bear. Poking a bear would provoke an attack. This is why we use the phrase "poking the bear." This is often used negatively to refer to annoying or antagonizing someone to get a response. The response is usually anger. But what does this have to do with love? Hebrews 10:24 says that we should "consider how we may provoke one another toward love and good deeds." As a Christian, whenever you are fellowshipping with other believers, you should either be provoked or the provoker.

Whether you're around a friend, family member, or someone who attends your local church, you should speak words that cause them to respond with love for others; this love should be reflected in good deeds. Your words may cause someone to be kind to a person that they have misjudged or convince someone to reconcile with a parent or sibling. Overall, as you go throughout your day, remember that provoking your neighbor is loving your neighbor.

🔍 Reflection

- According to the reading, what should Christians provoke one another to do?

- What are some ways that you can provoke your fellow brothers and sisters daily?

As you go throughout your day, remember that provoking your neighbor is loving your neighbor.

Day 19 Notes:

Day 19 Notes:

LOVE FOR PEOPLE: SECTION 3

Day 20 - "I'll Pray for You"

I thank my God every time I remember you. In all my prayers for all of you, I always pray with joy. **Philippians 1:3-4**

💡 Devotional Thought

One of the most loving acts that you can do for others around you is to pray for them. Prayer is more than just communication with God. Prayer is asking for God's blessing or involvement in a situation. However, we must remember that God responds to people and prayer however He chooses. I know what it's like to witness a situation you feel is beyond your ability to fix or change. In those cases, we pray to God for His involvement.

Sometimes, God's way of getting involved is by speaking to the hearts of other people to do something that helps the situation; however, we don't just pray for others during bad times, but we should also pray for them during good times. If things are going well, we pray that God continues to bless them. If they are growing in their faith or have obtained a new job opportunity, we pray that they will continue to grow and succeed in all that they do so that God is glorified. Praying for your neighbor is loving your neighbor.

🔍 Reflection

- Why should we pray for others?

- Should praying for your neighbor include praying for your enemies?

> Praying for your neighbor is loving your neighbor.

Day 20 Notes:

Day 20 Notes:

LOVE FOR PEOPLE: SECTION 3

Day 21 – Forgive One Another

> *Be kind and compassionate to one another, forgiving each other, just as in Christ God forgave you.* **Ephesians 4:32**

💡 Devotional Thought

One of the most difficult things to do in life is forgive. Paul teaches us in Ephesians 4:32 that we are to be kind and compassionate toward one another, forgiving one another as Christ has forgiven us. What does he mean by "as Christ has forgiven us"? We have been freely forgiven by Christ. It is not something that we have earned, nor do we deserve. Forgiveness is not a reward that we give to someone for their apology or change of actions; it is something that we freely choose to do. Yes, forgiveness is a choice, not a feeling. Also, forgiveness is not a one-time decision. We must decide to forgive every day even if we don't feel like it.

One simple way to do this is by praying, "Father, I forgive (person's name)," and then praying for God's best for that person. Forgiveness is not just letting go of what someone said or did to us; it is also freeing ourselves from an unhappy life of anger and bitterness. Forgiveness is how we love our neighbor.

🔍 Reflection

- How does unforgiveness affect our love for God and others?

- How often should we forgive?

> Forgiveness is how we love our neighbor.

Day 21 Notes:

Day 21 Notes:

LOVE FOR PEOPLE: SECTION 3

Day 22 - Encouragement

> *Therefore encourage one another and build each other up, just as in fact you are doing.* **1 Thessalonians 5:11**

💡 Devotional Thought

Every once in a while, we all need encouragement. Sometimes, we need to hear words like the following: "I'm proud of you!" "Keep going!" "God is with you!" "You will get through this!" or "I believe in you!" Discouragement can come from failure, negative words from others or ourselves, losing a family member, betrayal, etc. We all need people around us who can give us comforting and uplifting words when we feel down or defeated. Sometimes, we need encouragement to keep going when we are experiencing the temptation to quit doing something that truly matters. Other times, we need encouragement to continue to abstain or stay away from things that hinder us from being all that God has called and created us to be.

However, it's one thing to receive encouragement; it's another to encourage others. Part of loving your neighbor is encouraging your neighbor. Sometimes you may feel as if you don't have the perfect words of encouragement and that's fine. Sometimes just being present is in itself encouraging. Go out and love people today by encouraging someone!

🔍 Reflection

- How important is it to encourage others?

- Find someone to encourage today!

> Go out and love people today by encouraging someone!

Day 22 Notes:

Day 22 Notes:

LOVE FOR PEOPLE: SECTION 3

Day 23 - Sticks and Stones!

> *Do not let any unwholesome talk come out of your mouths, but only what is helpful for building others up according to their needs, that it may benefit those who listen.* **Ephesians 4:29**

💡 Devotional Thought

Growing up, I often heard people say, "Sticks and stones may break my bones, but words will never hurt me." As a kid, I remember thinking to myself, "Well, that's not true." Negative words can and really do hurt. I've spoken with adults who have held on to negative words that were spoken to them in their childhood and it has affected how they see themselves and hindered them from making meaningful connections with others.

How we talk to people matters. The Bible teaches us to build one another up rather than tear each other down with our words. Loving your neighbor means being mindful of the words that you speak to others. Positive words are just as powerful as negative words. Positive and godly words can convince people to begin to see themselves the way that Christ sees them. It is possible to speak such life-giving words today that impact someone's tomorrow!

🔍 Reflection

- What are some ways that you can build others up?

- Are you aware of how you talk to people, and are there areas where you can improve?

> It is possible to speak
> such life-giving words
> today that impact
> someone's tomorrow!

Day 23 Notes:

Day 23 Notes:

LOVE FOR PEOPLE: SECTION 3

Day 24- Love on the Streets

> *All they asked was that we should continue to remember the poor, the very thing I had been eager to do all along.* **Galatians 2:10**

💡 Devotional Thought

Jesus told His disciples, "The poor you will have with you always." The Bible teaches us to give to the poor or needy when we are able to. In Galatians 2:10, Paul says that he was eager to remember the poor! This doesn't mean that we give to every single homeless person that we meet. Sometimes these moments are prompted by the Holy Spirit, other times they are not. Prompted or not, opportunities to help the poor and needy are opportunities to love others. We show our love for others by helping to meet their spiritual and (at times) physical needs.

When we demonstrate love in this manner, we extend the love of God to those who may be financially or materially less fortunate. Sometimes God's way of meeting a need is through someone kind and compassionate enough to be the hands and feet of Jesus. Even if you can't help meet the physical needs of others, pray that God will send someone who will.

🔍 Reflection

- According to today's reading, what are two types of needs that we can help meet for others?

- How will you extend the love of God today?

Even if you can't help meet the physical needs of others, pray that God will send someone who will.

Day 24 Notes:

Day 24 Notes:

LOVE FOR PEOPLE: SECTION 3

Day 25 - Hit the Share Button!

> *"He said to them, 'Go into all the world and preach the gospel to all creation."* **Mark 16:15**

💡 Devotional Thought

One of the most loving things you could do for someone is share your faith with them. Remember, love must be genuine. Sharing your faith is not about trying to back someone into a corner and force them to receive Jesus as Savior and Lord so that you can add another person to your developing list of salvations. The goal is to genuinely engage in conversation with people and if the door swings open to share your faith, boldly and lovingly share the gospel with them.

Sharing your faith isn't limited to face-to-face conversations, you could even use your social media to spread or show the love of God and tell others the good news of Jesus Christ. There are times when we you may even want to look for ways to participate in an intentional outreach with a local church/ministry where the primary goal is to lead people to Jesus. Even during these times, be sure that your brief interactions are genuine and filled with God's love and truth. Start today, and go share your faith with someone!

🔍 Reflection

- According to today's reading, what are two types of needs that we can help meet for others?

- How will you extend the love of God today?

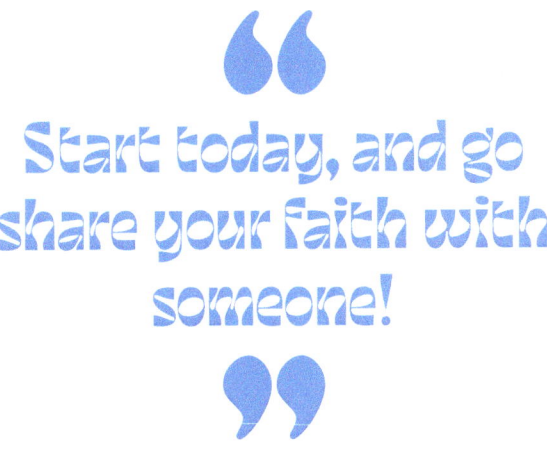

> Start today, and go share your faith with someone!

Day 25 Notes:

Day 25 Notes:

LOVE FOR PEOPLE: SECTION 3

Day 26 – You Should be Religious.

> *Religion that God our Father accepts as pure and faultless is this: to look after orphans and widows in their distress and to keep oneself from being polluted by the world.* **James 1:27**

💡 Devotional Thought

In the Western world, the word "religious" is a term that carries a lot of baggage. Not many people like to refer to themselves as religious, especially Christians. Most Christians use the phrase, "It's not about religion, it's about relationship. What if I told you that it is about religion and relationship with Jesus? James 1:27 talks about religion that God accepts as pure and genuine. The word "religion" in this verse means outward worship or devotion.

James tells us that God sees care for orphans and widows as pure and genuine worship unto Him. How can we do this? One way is by giving money to programs, ministries, and organizations that exist to help orphans or widows. Caring for them could also involve praying for them and/or visiting them if possible. As believers, our care for orphans and widows is not only another way that we worship God, but it is another way that we love our neighbor.

🔍 Reflection

- Is "religion," as mentioned in the Bible, bad?

- What does religion have to do with love for God and others?

As believers, our care for orphans and widows is not only another way that we worship God, but it is another way that we love our neighbor.

Day 26 Notes:

Day 26 Notes:

LOVE FOR PEOPLE: SECTION 3

Day 27 – What About my Enemies?

> *"But I tell you, love your enemies and pray for those who persecute you."* **Matthew 5:44**

💡 Devotional Thought

Should we love our enemies? The answer from Jesus is YES! Jesus says, "You have heard that it was said, 'Love your neighbor and hate your enemy.' But I tell you, love your enemies…" Why do you have to love your enemy? Because your enemy is still your neighbor. Certain people are not your enemies because they were created to be. They are your enemy because they choose to be.

Loving your enemy may be difficult, but you are more like your heavenly Father when you choose to love them. Loving them looks like praying for them or even helping them during a time of need. No matter who chooses to be our enemy, we should never want the worst for them. We should want God's best for them. Jesus goes further by asking the question "If you love those who love you, what reward will you get?" It's easy to love people who love you, but the true test of love is loving your enemies.

🔍 Reflection

- Is your enemy still your neighbor?

- What does it look like to love your enemies?

It's easy to love people who love you, but the true test of love is loving your enemies.

Day 27 Notes:

Day 27 Notes:

LOVE FOR PEOPLE: SECTION 3

Day 28 - Peace Out

> If it is possible, as far as it depends on you, live at peace with everyone. **Romans 12:18**

💡 Devotional Thought

Have you ever tried to get along with someone who disliked you? This person either disliked you for no reason or felt as if they had a valid reason for their dislike. Let me ask you another question: have you ever attempted to make amends with someone, and they refused? In life, it can be difficult to get along with people who have no desire to get along with you. In these cases, God doesn't hold it against us if we are unable to interact with certain people enough to extend love to them.

The Bible is not silent on this issue. Paul says, "If it is possible, as far as it depends on you, live at peace with everyone." Even Paul recognizes the difficulty of living peacefully with some people. So, what do we do? We love them by praying for them and, if possible, treating them the way we want to be treated, not the way they treat us. Love for your neighbor is being a peacemaker.

🔍 Reflection

- What should you do whenever it is difficult to make amends with someone who refuses?

- According to today's reading, "Love for your neighbor is being a _____."

Love for your neighbor is being a peacemaker.

Day 28 Notes:

Day 28 Notes:

LOVE FOR PEOPLE: SECTION 3

Day 29 - Tell the Truth!

> *Instead, speaking the truth in love, we will grow to become in every respect the mature body of him who is the head, that is, Christ.*
> **Ephesians 4:15**

💡 Devotional Thought

One of the hardest things for many people to do is be truthful. At times, we may avoid being truthful because of the possible consequences. Telling the truth may cost you a relationship/friendship, or even cause you to become hated and/or persecuted. Nevertheless, the truth helps far more than it initially hurts. The Bible teaches in Ephesians 4:15 to speak the truth in love. Some people will try to make you feel bad for speaking the truth by calling you judgmental or unloving.

Most times, this is their way of expressing their frustration and discomfort with confronting a part of their lives they don't want to deal with. What gives us the boldness to speak the truth in love is loving God more than we love ourselves and loving others more than we fear how they will respond to the truth. No matter what, never stop speaking the truth of God's word. You love your neighbor by speaking the truth to your neighbor.

🔍 Reflection

- According to Ephesians 4:15, how should we speak the truth?

- How would you respond to someone who calls you hateful and unloving because you speak the truth?

You love your neighbor
by speaking the truth to
your neighbor.

Day 29 Notes:

Day 29 Notes:

LOVE FOR PEOPLE: SECTION 3

Day 30 – Love God and Love People.

> *He answered: 'Love the Lord your God with all your heart and with all your soul and with all your strength and with all your mind; and, Love your neighbor as yourself.'* **Luke 10:27**

Devotional Thought

It is a beautiful and powerful thing to know that we are loved by God. It is even better when the love is mutual. That is, God loves us, and our response is love for Him. His love is not forced on us, nor does He force us to love Him. We express our love for Him in so many ways, and one of those ways is in how we love others. Loving others is what it means to be a true Christian.

We are more like Christ when we obey God's word and do unto others as we would have them do unto us. The goal is not just being loved but being love in a world filled with sin, hate, violence, injustice, and division. As Christians, our highest allegiance is to God and His word. Being a Christian means loving God more than we love anyone or anything else and loving our neighbor as ourselves.

Reflection

- What should be our response to God's love for us?

- According to the reading, "The goal is not just being _____ but being _____ in a sinful world."

> Love God and
> Love People.

Day 30 Notes:

Day 30 Notes:

Why 40?: SECTION 3

> Originally, this was going to be a 30-day devotional; however, after completing a class assignment on 1 John, I felt prompted by the Lord to include most of its content in this devotional. I'd like to refer to this part of the devotional as a bonus section. I pray that you enjoy these next **10 daily devotions** as we continue to grow our understanding of biblical love. Get ready to go deeper!

These Things: SECTION 4

Day 31 - These Things!

> I write these things to you who believe in the name of the Son of God so that you may know that you have eternal life. **1 John 5:13**

💡 Devotional Thought

While sitting in the McDonald's drive-thru, my wife turned to me with tears in her eyes and a face of sheer panic. I asked her what was bothering her, and she replied, "How do I know for sure that I have eternal life?" Believe it or not, many Christians struggle with assurance of their salvation. This struggle brings on feelings of unworthiness, anxiety, fear of God's judgment, and eternal separation from Him. My friend, as a believer, this is not how God desires us to live. He desires for us to live with the assurance that we have eternal life because we believe that Jesus is the Christ and the Son of God. **Eternal life** is a **gift** given to humanity that is the highest **expression** of **God's love**. In other words, God proves that **He loves us** by giving us eternal life.

John the Beloved wrote his epistle, 1 John, to assure fellow believers that they have eternal life because they have Jesus (5:13). John didn't write his epistle based on what he had been told by others but from firsthand experience. This is seen through his use of words such as "heard," "seen," and "touched" when speaking about the "Word of life" (1:1-3). In this way, he establishes his credibility so that he is more convincing to his readers. People who speak from experience tend to be the most convincing. It is as if John is saying to his readers, "Believe me, when it comes to the topic of eternal life, I know what I am talking about." He could not assure others if he lacked it within himself.

As I read 1 John 5:13, two words began to stick out to me: "These things!" That's how I came up with the title of this section. Then I began to ask myself: what exactly are "these things" within John's writing that are intended to assure his readers that they have eternal life? Does this refer to everything that he wrote up to this point, or does this refer to those things that are found only in Chapter 5? By reading the epistle carefully, I have come to realize that the phrase "these things" refers to things that are meant to assure believers that they have eternal life.

Reflection

- What is the highest expression of God's love for humanity?

- What does the assurance of our salvation have to do with God's love?

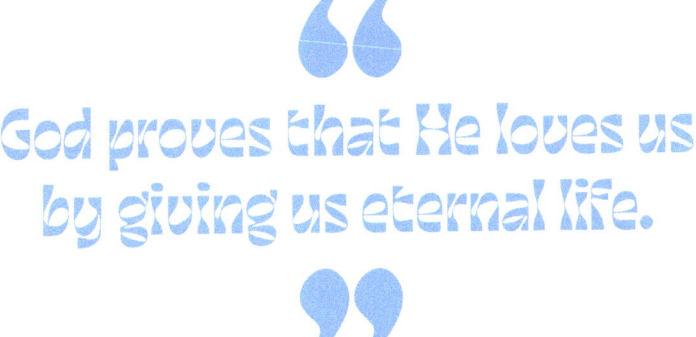

> God proves that He loves us by giving us eternal life.

Day 31 Notes:

Day 31 Notes:

These Things: SECTION 4

Day 32 – Lavishly Loved

> *See what great love the Father has lavished on us, that we should be called children of God! And that is what we are! 1 John 3:1*

💡 Devotional Thought

The Father has lavished His love on us and given us the privilege and status of sonship. In other words, we have undeservingly become children of God! This is our identity in Christ! What a beautiful spiritual reality this is! One of the ways that we embrace our identity is by choosing to live pure and not living in continual sin. Righteous living is how someone can tell the difference between the children of God and the children of the devil.

God's children have eternal life residing in them (3:1). Thus, God's adoption of us and our righteous living is an indication that we have eternal life. We are to live with the confidence that we are loved by God and that we belong to God. Our lives outwardly should reflect our inward spiritual reality. God has demonstrated His love for us by sending Jesus as an atoning sacrifice for sins (4:10). John teaches us that, as a result, the love of God should compel us to love one another (4:11).

🔍 Reflection

- What have we become as a result of God's love by receiving eternal life?

- What's the difference between the children of God and the children of the devil?

Our lives outwardly
should reflect our inward
spiritual reality.

Day 32 Notes:

Day 32 Notes:

These Things: SECTION 4

Day 33 – God's Children's Love

> *Anyone who hates a brother or sister is a murderer, and you know that no murderer has eternal life residing in him.* ***1 John 3:15***

Devotional Thought

John communicates to us that love for one another means that a believer has eternal life. Although equating hate to murder seems a bit extreme, John's point is clear: Those who have eternal life do not tolerate hatred because it does not care about the inherent value and well-being of others. God's children are willing to help their brothers or sisters. Because we have the love of God in us, we don't ignore the needs of others; instead, we help to meet their needs.

Whether they need food, finances, comfort, advice, encouragement, etc., our love for one another is our commitment to loving others with our words and actions and in truth. This type of love shows that God's love has grown within us and reached its highest potential (4:12). Our love for God and understanding His love for us influences how we love our family, friends, classmates, coworkers, etc.

Reflection

- According to John, what is love for others a sign of?

- A willingness to help others in need shows that God's love has done what in us?

Because we have the love of God in us, we don't ignore the needs of others; instead, we help to meet their needs.

Day 33 Notes:

Day 33 Notes:

These Things: SECTION 4

Day 34 – God's Children's Love Pt. 2

> *Dear friends, let us love one another, for love comes from God. Everyone who loves has been born of God and knows God.*
> ***1 John 4:7***

💡 Devotional Thought

Love for one another is a recurring theme throughout John's epistle. He is suggesting that love for others is one of the most obvious ways to tell that a believer has eternal life. Horizontal love is proof that God lives within His children. By loving one another, we prove that we are truly God's children and that we know Him. Knowing God is not to be confused with knowing "about" God. John is saying that our love for one another proves that we know God personally. When we truly know God's character and intentions, we are aware that He desires us to love others because He is love.

Believers who obey God's commands know Him personally, and their obedience proves that God's love has matured in them. John tells us that one of God's commands is love for one another (1 John 2:7; 3:11). He points out that love for brothers and sisters is how believers imitate Christ and show that they live in close fellowship with God. God's commands are not overwhelming to His children because they love Him and believe that Jesus is the Son of God. John explicitly states, "Everyone born of God overcomes the world" (1 John 5:4). But what does he mean by "overcomes the world"? To truly understand his words, it is important to consider what he wrote in 1 John 2:15-17. Here he wrote, "For everything in the world – the lust of the flesh, the lust of the eyes, and the pride of life – comes not from the Father but from the world." Thus, those of us who have become God's children (through belief in Jesus) do not give in to the temptations and attitudes of the world that hinder our love for God and one another.

🔍 Reflection

- What is a recurring theme throughout John's epistle?

- What does John mean by "Everyone born of God overcomes the world?"

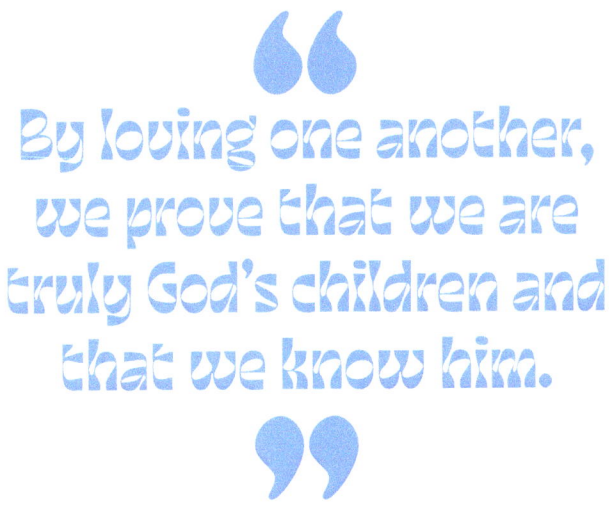

> By loving one another, we prove that we are truly God's children and that we know him.

Day 34 Notes:

Day 34 Notes:

These Things: SECTION 4

Day 35 - Mutual Indwelling Pt. 1

> *This is how we know that we live in Him and He in us: He has given us of His Spirit.* ***1 John 4:13***

💡 Devotional Thought

Have you ever said these words or heard someone else say them: "The feeling is mutual"? The idea is that two people feel the same way about something. As a child of God, the LIVING is mutual! God lives in us by His Spirit, and we live in Him by faith. In other words, we do life with God, and He lives His life through us!

We live in close connection with Him in an ongoing relationship of Father and child. It is His love for us and our love for Him and others that makes this possible. John gives us four marks of mutual indwelling: God has given His Spirit; God's children believe that Jesus is God's Son and the world's Savior; God's Children know and rely on God's love; Love for one another is a sign of mutual indwelling.

🔍 Reflection

- According to the reading, what is mutual indwelling?

- What are the four marks of mutual indwelling?

> We do life with God, and He lives His life through us!

Day 35 Notes:

Day 35 Notes:

These Things: SECTION 4

Day 36 - Mutual Indwelling Pt. 2

> *This is how love is made complete among us so that we will have confidence on the day of judgment: In this world, we are like Jesus.* ***1 John 4:17***

💡 Devotional Thought

John encourages believers to remain in this mutual relationship "so that when Christ appears, we may be confident and unashamed before Him at His coming" (1 John 2:28). What he is telling us through this verse and the rest of the chapter is that because living the right way is the outcome of this relationship, this increases our sense of belonging to Christ and confidence that we are righteous when he returns. The beauty of it is that God's love matures in His children through mutual indwelling and Christlikeness (1 John 4:16-17).

The maturity or completeness of God's love produces confidence on the day of judgment and drives out fear of experiencing His judgment (1 John 4:17-18). On judgment day, we can be confident that we have allowed His love to be perfected in us, which resulted in love for one another and confirmation of genuine love for God.

🔍 Reflection

- Why should Christians remain in a mutual relationship with Jesus?

- When God's love matures in us, what can we be confident of on the day of Judgment?

God's love matures in his children through mutual indwelling and Christ-likeness (1 John 4:16-17).

Day 36 Notes:

Day 36 Notes:

These Things: SECTION 4

Day 37 - Spiritual Certainties

> *I write these things to you who believe in the name of the Son of God so that you may know that you have eternal life.* **1 John 5:13**

💡 Devotional Thought

One thing that we can be certain of is that God loves us and has the best in mind for us! He desires that we live with the awareness and certainty of the benefits, privileges, and advantages that have become available to us because He demonstrated His love for us. In 1 John 2:12-14, he provides more ways to recognize that we have eternal life. He writes to his readers that their sins are forgiven, they know the Father and Son, they have overcome the evil one, and the word of God lives within them.

We should fully embrace and remind ourselves of these certainties whenever we are doubtful or questioning the eternal life that resides within us. Be confident today in who you are in Christ and what you have in Him! Don't let anyone or anything convince you otherwise. Live thankful and fully reliant on God and His love for you.

🔍 Reflection

- According to the reading, how can we be sure that we have eternal life?

- How do we keep ourselves aware of our spiritual reality without allowing life or other people to convince us otherwise?

> Live thankful and fully reliant on God and His love for you.

Day 37 Notes:

Day 37 Notes:

These Things: SECTION 4

Day 38 – Continuation in Community

> They went out from us, but they did not really belong to us. For if they had belonged to us, they would have remained with us; but their going showed that none of them belonged to us. **1 John 2:19**

💡 Devotional Thought

God's demonstration of love made it possible for us to live in a relationship with Him and to live in a healthy community with one another. Those who have eternal life have fellowship with the Father and their brothers and sisters in Christ (1 John 1:3). In other words, they prioritize cultivating vertical and horizontal relationships through their love for God and intentionally engaging in the faith community. Cultivating a relationship with God involves prayer, worship, and Bible reading. Faith community engagement could involve corporate worship gatherings, life groups, and attending social events.

Individuals who have eternal life residing in them are not easily led astray by antichrists (1 John 2:18-26). John suggests that the antichrists who departed from the faith community prove that they did not belong in the first place (1 John 2:18-19). Thus, eternal life is evident through continuation with the faith community. Moreover, John commends believers for maintaining their conviction that Jesus is the Christ and assures them that the anointing that resides in them is able to keep them from being led astray. As God's children, we rely on His word and the Spirit of God to give us the ability to discern false teachings that would encourage departure from the faith community. Our continued commitment to the faith community displays our love for God and one another.

🔍 Reflection

- According to today's reading, God's demonstration of His love made it possible for us to do what?

- What does our continued commitment to the faith community (church) say about us?

> Our continued commitment to the faith community displays our love for God and one another.

Day 38 Notes:

Day 38 Notes:

These Things: SECTION 4

Day 39 - Sin Less and be Sinless

💡 **Devotional Thought**

While reading a devotional about biblical love, you probably didn't expect to read an entry exclusively about sin, or maybe you did. However, John talks about it in his epistle. In one verse, he says, "If we claim to be without sin, we deceive ourselves, and the truth is not in us" (1 John 1:8). In another verse, he says, "No one who is born of God will continue to sin, because God's seed remains in them; they cannot go on sinning, because they have been born of God" (1 John 3:9). This sounds confusing! Do I live sinless or not? If I commit a sin, does that mean that I'm not saved? Have you ever done or said something wrong and felt bad about it, not simply because you knew it was wrong, but because you knew it was a sin against God, and it made you question your salvation? Let me help you, my friend. John is saying that none of us are perfect.

No human has reached sinless perfection other than Jesus. However, even though we know that we aren't perfect because we are God's children, we choose to confess to Him when we commit a sin, and we don't make sin a lifestyle. There's a difference between committing a sin (occasionally) and a commitment to sin.

As Christians, we are committed to God, not sin. Also, here's something to keep in mind: we must never allow a moment of sin to make us question our love for God and His love for us. We know we truly love God, not because we are sinless, but because we sin less.

🔍 Reflection

- According to the reading, what should genuine Christians do if they sin?

- What must we never allow sin to make us do to ourselves?

> We know we truly love God, not because we are sinless, but because we sin less.

Day 39 Notes:

Day 39 Notes:

These Things: SECTION 4

Day 40 - "as yourself"

> *Jesus replied: "'Love the Lord your God with all your heart and with all your soul and with all your mind.' This is the first and greatest commandment. And the second is like it: 'Love your neighbor as yourself.'"* **Matthew 22:37-39**

💡 Devotional Thought

Some Christians believe that it is "unchristian" to speak of self-love. Oftentimes, they have in mind a worldly understanding of self-love that expresses itself through arrogance, selfishness, and self-centeredness. But how can you truly love your neighbor "as yourself" if you don't love yourself? Biblically speaking, what does it mean to love yourself? Self-love begins with realizing that God considers you worthy of love (John 3:16; Romans 5:8 1 John 4:9-10). Self-love is also praising and thanking God for uniquely making you in a way that shows how awesome He is (Psalm 139:14). The fact that He created you in His image tells you how valuable you are (Genesis 1:27). You get to represent Him wherever you go. Self-love involves caring for and honoring God with your body (Ephesians 5:29; 1 Corinthians 6:19-20).

Lastly, those who love themselves love God, seek wisdom and understanding, and think humbly of themselves (Mark 12:30-31; Proverbs 19:8; Romans 12:3). As you continue your journey as a Christian, remember that there is a difference between biblical self-love and worldly self-love. If you struggle with loving yourself, remember that God considers you worthy of love, not because you've earned it, but because He chose to love you.

God considers you worthy of love, not because you've earned it, but because He chose to love you.

Day 40 Notes:

Day 40 Notes:

Self-Assessment

Double love is about loving God and loving others! Today is the day you do a self- assessment! I trust that you have applied what you've read and experienced transformation. Here are a few things to remember:

> 1. You are loved by God.
>
> 2. Receiving His love causes us to love Him back and to love others. Loving others can be challenging. Sometimes, it seems easier to love God than it is to love people. Even John knew this was a human tendency (1 John 4:20). But to love people is to love God. With a life devoted to God through prayer, Bible reading, and cooperation with the Holy Spirit, this becomes possible.

Now, let's see how much you've grown!

How's your love for God? How's your love for your neighbor? How do you know that your love for God and people has grown? Are there still areas for improvement? If so, what will you commit to doing so that you can continue to love on another level?

Take a moment and write about specific moments throughout this journey when you realized that your love for God and/or others **grew stronger**.

When it seems difficult to love people, what can we do so that it becomes easier?

What is **Double Love** about?

Consider ways that you can share what you've learned about "Double Love" with others.

> Double love is about loving God and loving others!

Self Assessment Notes:

Self Assessment Notes:

**Continue sharing your journey!
Follow and tag
#thedoublelovedevo**